# Unique Homemade Seasonings and Spices Cookbook

Seasoning Recipes to Enhance the Flavor of Your Meals

## BY

## MOLLY MILLS

Copyright © 2019 by Molly Mills

# License Notes

# An Amazing Offer for Buying My Book!

Thank you very much for purchasing my books! As a token of my appreciation, I would like to extend an amazing offer to you! When you have subscribed with your e-mail address, you will have the opportunity to get free and discounted e-books that will show up in your inbox daily. You will also receive reminders before an offer expires so you never miss out. With just little effort on your part, you will have access to the newest and most informative books at your fingertips. This is all part of the VIP treatment when you subscribe below.

**SIGN ME UP:** *https://molly.gr8.com*

# Table of Contents

# Chapter I: Barbecue Seasoning Recipes

AAAAAAAAAAAAAAAAAAAAAAAAAAAAAAAAAAAAAAAAAAAAAAAAA

# Recipe 1: Barbecue and Herbs Blend

The perfect mixture of barbecue flavor and herbs works well on lamb, beef, pork or any type of game meat.

**Makes:** 1 cup

**Total Prep Time:** 15 minutes

**List of Ingredients:**

- 1 ½ Tbsp. oregano
- 1 ½ Tbsp. basil
- 2 tsp. ground bay leaf
- ¼ cup savory
- ¼ cup juniper berries
- ¼ cup rosemary

AAAAAAAAAAAAAAAAAAAAAAAAAAAAAAAAAAAAAAAAAAAAAAAAA

**Methods:**

**1:** Place all the ingredients in a food processor or blender. Pulse until the ingredients are finely ground.

**2:** Store in an airtight container until ready to use.

# Recipe 2: Barbecue Seasoning

Use this seasoning for meats both on and off the grill.

**Makes:** 3 cups

**Total Prep Time:** 10 to 15 minutes

**List of Ingredients:**

- 3 tsp. ground cayenne pepper
- 6 Tbsp. ground black pepper, coarse
- 6 Tbsp. salt, table or kosher
- 6 Tbsp. chili powder, dark
- 6 Tbsp. cumin
- 12 Tbsp. paprika
- 12 Tbsp. sugar, granulated

AAAAAAAAAAAAAAAAAAAAAAAAAAAAAAAAAAAAAAAAAAAAAAA

**Methods:**

**1:** Mix all the ingredients together until well combined.

**2:** Transfer the seasoning mix into an airtight container and store in a cool, dry location.

# Chapter II: Curry Seasoning Recipes

AAAAAAAAAAAAAAAAAAAAAAAAAAAAAAAAAAAAAAAAAAAAAAAAA

# Recipe 3: Simple Curry Rice Spice

This two-ingredient curry spice can be made into a flavor packet for use on rice.

**Makes:** 1

**Total Prep Time:** 20 to 30 minutes

**List of Ingredients:**

- 1 tsp. curry powder
- 3 cubes chicken bouillon

AAAAAAAAAAAAAAAAAAAAAAAAAAAAAAAAAAAAAAAAAAAAAAAA

**Methods:**

**1:** Crush the chicken bouillon cubes into a fine powder.

**2:** Mix the crush bouillon cubes with the curry powder. Store in an airtight container until ready to use.

**3:** When ready to use, simply add the entire mix to the water when you are cooking the rice.

# Recipe 4: Traditional Indian Curry Recipe

This traditional Indian curry seasoning has medium-hot heat and can be used whenever a recipe calls for curry powder.

**Makes:** Makes 1 ¼ cups

**Total Prep Time:** 35 to 60 minutes

**List of Ingredients:**

- 6 red chilies, dried and seeds removed
- 2 tsp. cumin seeds
- 1 ounce coriander seeds
- 1 tsp. black peppercorns
- 1 tsp. fenugreek seeds
- ½ tsp. mustard seeds
- 10 curry leaves, fresh
- 1 Tbsp. turmeric, ground
- ½ tsp. ginger, ground

AAAAAAAAAAAAAAAAAAAAAAAAAAAAAAAAAAAAAAAAAAAAAAAAA

**Methods:**

**1:** After removing the seeds from the red chilies, dry roast all the spices on the stove over medium heat. Continue roasting until they have darkened. Make sure to shake or stir frequently to keep the spices from burning. Remove the pan from the stove and let cool.

**2:** Place all the roasted ingredients in a food processor and grind into a powder.

**3:** Store the curry powder in an airtight container until ready to use.

# Recipe 5: African-Style Curry Powder for Vegetables

This African-style curry powder is designed for use on vegetables and will give even the blandish dish a much-needed boost.

**Makes:** Makes 2 ½ cups

**Total Prep Time:** 15 to 25 minutes

**List of Ingredients:**

- 1 cup red chilies, dried
- 1 tsp. black pepper
- 1 cup coriander
- ¼ cup turmeric
- 1 tsp. mustard seeds
- 1 tsp. cumin
- 1 tsp. fenugreek
- 1 tsp. green gram dhal
- 1 tsp. black gram dhal
- 2 tsp. Bengal gram dhal

AAAAAAAAAAAAAAAAAAAAAAAAAAAAAAAAAAAAAAAAAAAAAAAAAA

**Methods:**

**1:** Place all the spices in a food processor and grind into a powder. Store in an airtight container.

**2:** When ready to use, sprinkle on vegetables at a rate of 2 tsp. for every half pound of vegetables.

# Chapter III: Common Kitchen Spice Mix Recipes

AAAAAAAAAAAAAAAAAAAAAAAAAAAAAAAAAAAAAAAAAAAAA

# Recipe 6: All-Purpose Herb Seasoning

This all-purpose herb seasoning has a wide array of uses, from seasoning chicken to adding flavor to salads.

**Makes:** 1/3 cup

**Total Prep Time:** 12 minutes

**List of Ingredients:**

- ¼ tsp. lemon peel, dried
- 1 tsp. oregano
- 1 tsp. celery seed
- 2 Tbsp. onion powder
- 2 Tbsp. basil
- Dash of black pepper

AAAAAAAAAAAAAAAAAAAAAAAAAAAAAAAAAAAAAAAAAAAAAAAAAA

**Methods:**

**1:** Mix all the ingredients together.

**2:** Transfer the herb seasoning into an airtight container. Store in a cool dry location until ready to use.

# Recipe 7: Seasoned Salt

Seasoned salt is a kitchen staple and can be used in a wide array of dishes and recipes.

**Makes:** 10 ½ tsp.

**Total Prep Time:** 15 minutes

**List of Ingredients:**

- ¼ tsp. turmeric
- ¼ tsp. asoefetida
- ¼ tsp. caraway
- ¼ tsp. coriander
- ½ tsp. rosemary
- ½ tsp. marjoram
- ½ tsp. ground cumin
- ½ tsp. thyme
- ½ tsp. parsley
- ½ tsp. ground black pepper
- ½ tsp. cayenne pepper
- 1 tsp. salt, table or kosher
- 1 tsp. oregano
- 1 tsp. dill

- 1 tsp. celery, dried
- 2 tsp. paprika

AAAAAAAAAAAAAAAAAAAAAAAAAAAAAAAAAAAAAAAAAAAAA

**Methods:**

**1:** Combine all the ingredients together.

**2:** Store in an airtight container. Place in a cool, dry location where the container is out of direct sunlight and away from direct heat.

# Recipe 8: Fish Seasoning

Use this blend to seasoning any type of fish.

**Makes:** 3 cups

**Total Prep Time:** 15 minutes

**List of Ingredients:**

- 1 tsp. chives, dried
- 1 Tbsp. thyme
- 1 Tbsp. marjoram
- 1 Tbsp. celery seed
- 1 Tbsp. savory, dried
- 1 Tbsp. grated lemon rind, dried
- 2 Tbsp. parsley flakes
- 1 bay leaf

**Methods:**

**1:** Break the bay leaf into small pieces and place inside a bowl.

**2:** Add the remaining ingredients to the bowl and mix until thoroughly combined.

**3:** Transfer the seasoning to an airtight container and store in a cool dry location until ready to use.

# Recipe 9: Italian Seasoning

Italian seasoning is perfect for any recipe where you want to add the classic tastes of Italy.

**Makes:** 1 cup

**Total Prep Time:** 15 minutes

**List of Ingredients:**

- 2 Tbs. oregano
- 2 Tbs. basil
- 2 Tbs. Coriander leaf
- 2 Tbs. Marjoram
- 2 Tbs. rosemary
- 2 Tbs. Savory
- 2 Tbs. Thyme
- 1 tsp. red pepper flakes

AAAAAAAAAAAAAAAAAAAAAAAAAAAAAAAAAAAAAAAAAAAAAAAAAA

**Methods:**

**1:** Place all the herbs into a food processor. Pulse the ingredients together for about 35 seconds or until the ingredients are ground.

**2:** Place the Italian seasoning is an airtight container and store in a dry, dark location until ready to use.

# Recipe 10: Bay Seafood Seasoning

Despite its name, this bay seafood seasoning recipe can be used on chicken as well as any type of seafood.

**Makes:** ¼ cup

**Total Prep Time:** 15 minutes

**List of Ingredients:**

- 1 Tbsp. bay leaves, ground
- 2 ½ tsp. celery salt
- ¾ tsp. nutmeg, ground
- 1 ½ tsp. black pepper, ground
- 1 ½ tsp. dry mustard
- ½ tsp. cloves, ground
- ½ tsp. paprika
- ½ tsp. ginger, ground
- ½ tsp. red pepper
- ¼ tsp. cardamom, ground (optional)
- ¼ tsp. mace, ground (optional)

AAAAAAAAAAAAAAAAAAAAAAAAAAAAAAAAAAAAAAAAAAAAAAAA

**Methods:**

**1:** Mix all the ingredients together for several seconds until thoroughly combined.

**2:** Store the blend in an airtight container.

# Recipe 11: Pizza Seasoning

Forgo that commercial pizza seasoning and instead use this homemade blend that tastes just as good if not better than its massed produced counterpart.

**Makes:** 1/2 cup

**Total Prep Time:** 10 minutes

**List of Ingredients:**

- ½ Tbsp. coarsely ground black pepper
- ½ Tbsp. ginger
- ½ Tbsp. lemon peel in dried form
- ½ Tbsp. paprika
- ½ Tbsp. onion flakes, dried
- ½ Tbsp. fennel
- ½ Tbsp. thyme
- ½ Tbsp. garlic powder
- 1 Tbsp. basil
- 2 Tbsp. oregano

AAAAAAAAAAAAAAAAAAAAAAAAAAAAAAAAAAAAAAAAAAAAAAAA

**Methods:**

**1:** Place all the ingredients in an airtight container. Secure the lid on the container.

**2:** Shake the container for several seconds until the ingredients are well combined. Store in a cool, dry location until ready to use.

# Recipe 12: All-Purpose Salt Substitute Blend

This salt substitute blend is ideal for individuals who cannot have salt or those who are looking to reduce their total sodium intake.

**Makes:** 2 Tbsp.

**Total Prep Time:** 10 minutes

**List of Ingredients:**

- 1 tsp. oregano
- 1 tsp. dillweed
- 1 tsp. lemon rind, powdered
- 1 tsp. basil
- 2 tsp. garlic powder

AAAAAAAAAAAAAAAAAAAAAAAAAAAAAAAAAAAAAAAAAAAAAAA

**Methods:**

**1:** Blend the ingredients together until well incorporated into one another.

**2:** Pour the blend in a glass salt shaker. Place a couple of rice grains inside to help prevent the spice from caking.

**3:** Use as a substitute for salt.

# Recipe 13: Poultry Seasoning

This spice blend works best in stuffing or in recipes where poultry seasoning is called for.

**Makes:** 1 serving

**Total Prep Time:** 10 minutes

**List of Ingredients:**

- ½ tsp. nutmeg
- 1 Tbsp. rosemary
- 1 Tbsp. black pepper
- 1 Tbsp. marjoram
- 1 Tbsp. savory, dried
- 2 Tbsp. thyme
- 2 Tbsp. parsley
- 2 Tbsp. sage

AAAAAAAAAAAAAAAAAAAAAAAAAAAAAAAAAAAAAAAAAAAAAAAA

**Methods:**

**1:** Blend all the ingredients together and store in an airtight container until ready to use.

# Chapter IV: Greek Seasoning Recipes

AAAAAAAAAAAAAAAAAAAAAAAAAAAAAAAAAAAAAAAAAAAAAAAAAA

# Recipe 14: Greek Blend Seasoning

This blend is filled with Greek-style flavor and can be used on pork chops, fish, steak and chicken.

**Makes:** ¼ cup

**Total Prep Time:** 15 minutes

**List of Ingredients:**

- 2 tsp. dried oregano
- 2 tsp. table salt
- 1 ½ tsp. garlic powder
- 1 ½ tsp. onion powder
- 1 tsp. dried parsley flakes
- 1 tsp. cornstarch
- 1 tsp. beef bouillon granules
- 1 tsp. black pepper
- ½ tsp. nutmeg
- ½ tsp. cinnamon

AAAAAAAAAAAAAAAAAAAAAAAAAAAAAAAAAAAAAAAAAAAAAAAAAA

**Methods:**

**1:** Place all ingredients in an airtight container.

**2:** Secure the lid and shake vigorously for several seconds until all ingredients are well incorporated with one another.

**3:** Store the blend-filled container in a cool, dry location until ready to use.

# Recipe 15: Geek-Inspired Lemon Seasoning

This Greek-inspired lemon seasoning recipe can be used on beef, lamb, rice or any other dish where you want the perfect combination of Greek and lemon flavors.

**Makes:** 8 tsp.

**Total Prep Time:** 10 minutes

**List of Ingredients:**

- 2 tsp. lemon pepper
- 2 tsp. garlic salt
- 2 tsp. mint, dried
- 2 tsp. oregano

AAAAAAAAAAAAAAAAAAAAAAAAAAAAAAAAAAAAAAAAAAAAAAAAA

**Methods:**

**1:** Mix all the ingredients together and store in an airtight container until ready to use.

# Recipe 16: Traditional Greek Seasoning

This recipe can be used in replace of any Greek seasoning called for in any recipe.

**Makes:** 1 ¾ tsp.

**Total Prep Time:** 10 minutes

**List of Ingredients:**

- ½ tsp. cumin
- ¼ tsp. black pepper
- ¼ tsp. paprika
- ¾ tsp. Greek oregano
- 1 tsp. minced garlic, dried
- 1 pinch table salt

AAAAAAAAAAAAAAAAAAAAAAAAAAAAAAAAAAAAAAAAAAAAAAAAAA

**Methods:**

**1:** Combine all the ingredients together.

**2:** Store in an airtight container until ready to use.

# Chapter V: Cajun Spice Mix Recipes

AAAAAAAAAAAAAAAAAAAAAAAAAAAAAAAAAAAAAAAAAAAAAAA

# Recipe 17: Dynamite Dust

This Cajun seasoning mix has a bit more heat and can be used whenever you want to add some kick to a recipe.

**Makes:** Makes 2 ½ cups

**Total Prep Time:** 15 to 20 minutes

**List of Ingredients:**

- 6 Tbsp. salt, kosher
- 3 Tbsp. dried basil
- ½ cup paprika
- ¼ cup black pepper, ground coarsely
- 2 Tbsp. garlic powder
- 2 Tbsp. oregano, dried
- 2 Tbsp. onion powder
- 2 Tbsp. dry mustard
- 3 Tbsp. gumbo files powder
- 2 Tbsp. cayenne pepper
- 2 Tbsp. thyme, dried
- 2 Tbsp. white pepper

AAAAAAAAAAAAAAAAAAAAAAAAAAAAAAAAAAAAAAAAAAAAAAAAA

**Methods:**

**1:** Combine all the ingredients together in an airtight container. Store in a dark, cool and dry location.

# Recipe 18: Traditional Cajun Seasoning

This recipe creates the traditional Cajun taste that can be found in a wide array of cultural dishes

**Makes:** 1

**Total Prep Time:** 20 minutes

**List of Ingredients:**

- 2 ½ tsp. table salt
- 1 Tbsp. sweet paprika
- 1 tsp. garlic powder
- 1 tsp. onion powder
- 1 tsp. cayenne powder
- ¾ tsp. black pepper
- ¾ tsp. white pepper
- ½ tsp. thyme leaves, dried

AAAAAAAAAAAAAAAAAAAAAAAAAAAAAAAAAAAAAAAAAAAAAAAAAA

**Methods:**

**1:** Mix all the ingredients together until well combined. Store the spice mix in an airtight container.

# Recipe 19: Cajun Herb Seasoning Mix

The perfect mixture of Cajun spice and traditional herbs creates a well-rounded seasoning mix that you can use on just about any meat or poultry.

**Makes:** 1

**Total Prep Time:** 20 minutes

**List of Ingredients:**

- 2 Tbsp. minced onion, dried
- 2 Tbsp. minced garlic, dried
- 5 Tbsp. paprika
- 1 Tbsp. cayenne pepper
- 1 ½ tsp. white pepper
- 1 ½ tsp. oregano, dried
- 1 ½ tsp. basil, dried

ΛΛΛΛΛΛΛΛΛΛΛΛΛΛΛΛΛΛΛΛΛΛΛΛΛΛΛΛΛΛΛΛΛΛΛΛΛΛΛΛΛΛΛΛΛΛΛΛΛΛΛ

**Methods:**

**1:** Mix all the ingredients together in an airtight container. The mixture can be stored in a cool, dry location for up to 6 months.

**2:** When ready to use, rub or sprinkle the seasoning over the desired meat or poultry and cook as you normally would.

# Recipe 20: Cajun Seasoning Rub for Chicken

This spicy rub recipe will turn that dull chicken into a mouthwatering flavor-experience that you will want to revisit regularly.

**Makes:** 1

**Total Prep Time:** 35 minutes

**List of Ingredients:**

- ½ tsp. cayenne pepper
- 1 tsp. ground black pepper
- ½ tsp. cumin, ground
- ½ tsp. white pepper
- ½ tsp. table salt
- ½ tsp. nutmeg, ground
- 2 Tbsp. vegetable oil

AAAAAAAAAAAAAAAAAAAAAAAAAAAAAAAAAAAAAAAAAAAAAAAAA

**Methods:**

**1:** Mix everything but the vegetable oil together in a small bowl.

**2:** Pour 1 Tbsp. of the oil in a small bowl. Use a brush to brush the oil onto both sides of the chicken.

**3:** Rub the spice mixture from 1 all over the entire chicken.

**4:** Pour the remaining 1 Tbsp. of vegetable into a large skillet and set on the stove over medium heat.

**5:** Cook the chicken as you normally would in the heated skillet for about 10 minutes or until there is no pink inside.

# Chapter VI: Taco Seasoning Recipes

AAAAAAAAAAAAAAAAAAAAAAAAAAAAAAAAAAAAAAAAAAAAAAAA

# Recipe 21: Low Sodium Taco Seasoning

This recipe contains no salt, thus making it a perfect choice for those people who are looking to reduce the amount of sodium in their daily.

**Makes:** 5 tsp.

**Total Prep Time:** 10 minutes

**List of Ingredients:**

- 1 tsp. red pepper flakes
- 1 tsp. cumin
- 3 tsp. chili powder

AAAAAAAAAAAAAAAAAAAAAAAAAAAAAAAAAAAAAAAAAAAAAAAAA

**Methods:**

**1:** Mix the three ingredients together in an airtight container. Seasoning the meat to taste with this low sodium taco blend.

# Recipe 22: Spicy Spicy Taco Mix

For when you want something a bit spicier than traditional taco seasoning, use the following recipe.

**Makes:** 2 Tbsp.

**Total Prep Time:** 10 minutes

**List of Ingredients:**

- 1 tsp. chili powder
- 1 tsp. table salt
- ½ tsp. cornstarch
- ½ tsp. dried red pepper, crushed
- ½ tsp. cumin
- ½ tsp. garlic, instant minced
- ¼ tsp. oregano, dried
- 2 tsp. onion, instant minced

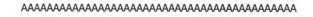

AAAAAAAAAAAAAAAAAAAAAAAAAAAAAAAAAAAAAAAAAAAAAAAA

**Methods:**

**1:** Blend all the ingredients together in an airtight container.

**2:** Use in place of 1 package of commercial taco seasoning.

# Recipe 23: Traditional Taco Seasoning

Why purchase commercial taco seasoning when you can make your own using the following recipe.

**Makes:** ½ cup

**Total Prep Time:** 10 minutes

**List of Ingredients:**

- 5 tsp. paprika
- 3 tsp. onion powder
- 6 tsp. chili powder
- 4 ½ tsp. paprika
- 1/8 tsp. cayenne pepper
- 2 ½ tsp. garlic powder

AAAAAAAAAAAAAAAAAAAAAAAAAAAAAAAAAAAAAAAAAAAAAAAA

**Methods:**

**1:** Dump the herbs and spices into a container with a lid. Using a stirring utensil, mix all the herbs and spices together.

**2:** Use 7 tsp. of the taco seasoning for every 1.25 ounce package, which is the typical weight of commercially available, mass produced taco mix.

# Chapter VII: Dessert Spice Mix Recipes

AAAAAAAAAAAAAAAAAAAAAAAAAAAAAAAAAAAAAAAAAAAAAAA

# Recipe 24: Pumpkin Pie Spice

Who doesn't love the flavor of pumpkin pie? And with this spice blend, you can bring the taste of that Thanksgiving staple to anything and everything!

**Makes:** ½ cup

**Total Prep Time:** 10 to 15 minutes

**List of Ingredients:**

- 1 tsp. cloves, ground
- 1 ½ tsp. nutmeg, ground
- 1 ½ tsp. ginger, ground
- 1 Tbsp. allspice, ground
- ¼ cup cinnamon, ground

AAAAAAAAAAAAAAAAAAAAAAAAAAAAAAAAAAAAAAAAAAAAAAA

**Methods:**

**1:** Mix the 5 ingredients together and store in an airtight jar.

# Recipe 25: Apple Pie Spice

This spice mix can be used in everything from dessert recipes to your morning tea.

**Makes:** 2 servings

**Total Prep Time:** 10 minutes

**List of Ingredients:**

- ¼ tsp. cloves, ground
- 1 tsp. allspice, ground
- 1 ½ tsp. nutmeg, ground
- 1 Tbsp. cinnamon, ground

AAAAAAAAAAAAAAAAAAAAAAAAAAAAAAAAAAAAAAAAAAAAAAAA

**Methods:**

**1:** Combine all the ingredients together in an airtight container.

**2:** Use the seasoning to taste.

# Chapter VIII: Benefits of Making your own Seasoning and Spice Blends

Now, I'm sure it may have crossed your mind that it would just be so much easier to go to the store and purchase commercially produced seasoning mixes and spice blends. After all, stores have a wide array of these mixes and blends readily available and right at your fingertips.

AAAAAAAAAAAAAAAAAAAAAAAAAAAAAAAAAAAAAAAAAAAAAAAAA

# (1) Complete Control Over the Ingredients

Take a look at the ingredient lists of commercially produced seasoning mixes and spice blends. You will find a wide array of fillers, like anti-caking ingredients, MSG and sugar. These unnecessary ingredients can lead to food intolerance and allergies that pose a threat to yourself and your family. When you make your own spices and blends, you can choose to not include the unwanted ingredients and use a more suitable substitute.

AAAAAAAAAAAAAAAAAAAAAAAAAAAAAAAAAAAAAAAAAAAAAAAAAA

# (2) Saves You Money

As I am sure you know, spice blends cost, at the very least, twice as much as single spices, which can be purchased in bulk to lower their price even more. If there is a spice blend that you use regularly, you could be spending hundreds of dollars a year just keeping that blend on hand. Making your own seasoning and blends greatly reduce the costs, thus saving you money.

AAAAAAAAAAAAAAAAAAAAAAAAAAAAAAAAAAAAAAAAAAAAAAAAA

# (1) Saves You Time

You're probably thinking, "how can taking time out of your busy schedule to make spice blends actually save you time?" It's simple really. When you make your own spice blends, you are more likely to keep them on hand. And when you have them on hand, there is no need to make a run to the store.

AAAAAAAAAAAAAAAAAAAAAAAAAAAAAAAAAAAAAAAAAAAAAAAAAA

# (1) More Health Benefits

Making your own spice blends provide you with more health benefits than what you could get with commercially available blends and seasonings. Spices can actually have a major impact on your overall health and well-being, sometimes without you even knowing it. From lowering fevers, to improving digestion and even reducing inflammation, homemade spice blends can help keep your physical and mental health in check. Now, I'm sure you are wondering why the blends in the store cannot give you the same benefit. It all lies within the freshness. When the freshness is gone from the seasoning, it loses its potency. And since you cannot be sure just how fresh those store bought blends are, you are probably not getting the maximum benefits that spices provide.

AAAAAAAAAAAAAAAAAAAAAAAAAAAAAAAAAAAAAAAAAAAAAAAAA

# (1) The Ability to Customize the Mixes and Blends

When you create your own blends and seasonings, you can play around with ingredients. If you don't like cloves, for example, you can eliminate them from the pumpkin pie spice recipe and replace it with a bit more allspice. And this is perfect for people who suffer from food allergies, you simply remove the offending ingredient from the recipe. Making your own seasoning blends and spice mixes gives you the freedom to customize any recipe a little or a lot to suit your specific needs and desires.

AAAAAAAAAAAAAAAAAAAAAAAAAAAAAAAAAAAAAAAAAAAAAAAAAA

# (2) Mixes and Blends are Fresher

Those containers of commercially available mixes and blends could have been sitting on the shelf of the store for far too long. When you make the mix yourself, you can clearly write the date on the container so you can ensure that you are always uses the freshest blend possible.

# (3) Satisfy Picky Eaters

Picky eaters, especially children, can make meal time a frustrating experience. Homemade seasonings and blends, however, let you change the flavor of foods, making them more desirable to those picky eaters. Simply take the flavors that they love and create a blend just for them. Sprinkle this blend on foods that your picky eater doesn't particularly like, such as vegetables, and voila! You have a dish that even the pickiest of eaters will enjoy.

AAAAAAAAAAAAAAAAAAAAAAAAAAAAAAAAAAAAAAAAAAAAAAAAAA

# (4) Homemade Spices and Blends Make A Great Gift

Your own homemade spices and blends make a wonderful gift! And since they are relatively inexpensive to make, you don't need to break the bank to give your family and friends a unique gift that they will love. With that said, you shouldn't just give the spices and blends without putting any thought into it. Sit down and think of what type of seasoning the recipient would like. If you know they are fans of BBQ, make them a barbecue blend. Or, if they like baking yummy desserts, whip up apple spice or pumpkin spice seasoning. Furthermore, don't hand the recipient the spice mix in a plastic bag. Presentation is important and packaging the spice blend in a glass jar with a decorative ribbon tied around it will complete the entire look of the gift.

AAAAAAAAAAAAAAAAAAAAAAAAAAAAAAAAAAAAAAAAAAAAAAAAAA

# Chapter IX: Tools Needed to Create your Own Seasoning and Spice Blends

Not much is needed to create the seasoning and spice blends in this cookbook, as well as others. In fact, you probably have many, if not all, of the required tools to start filling your spice draw with your very own spice mixes and seasoning blends. And even you have don't have all the tools, you can find them in just about any store for a relatively inexpensive price.

To begin, you will need airtight containers, such as glass jars, where you can store your spice blends. Small mason jars work well to keep your seasoning and spice blends fresh. No matter what container you use, make sure it is cleaned and completely dried before placing the spice inside.

You will also need measuring spoons to measure out the spices, bowls and stirring utensils, such as spoons, to mix all the ingredients. And, of course, you will need spices!

AAAAAAAAAAAAAAAAAAAAAAAAAAAAAAAAAAAAAAAAAAAAAAAAAA

# (1) 10 Basic Spices

To draw on the above list, let's discuss 10 basic spices and what they are used for. This will help give you a better understanding of spices and their usage.

1.  **Paprika** – This spice is versatile and can be used in a wide array of dishes. Paprika works well on everything from vegetables to meats, and even commonly added to seafood recipes.

2.  **Cayenne Pepper** – This hot and spicy pepper is a kitchen favorite. It has a powerful spicy taste, so only a small amount is generally needed. While it works best in Indian and Cajun-style recipes, cayenne pepper can be added whenever you want a little humph to a dish.

3.  **Black Peppercorns** – This must have spice gives a pleasant flavor without the overbearingness often associated with pepper spices.

4.  **Ground Ginger** – Because it has a strong flavor, ginger is generally used in small does.

5. **Ground Cumin** – Cumin is the perfect combination of not too dull yet not too sweet. It is a common ingredient in Middle Eastern dishes and often found in Spanish and Mexican delicacies.

6. **Chili Powder** – This well-known spice is found in recipes all over the world. Chili powder typically consists of a blend of cumin, dried chili peppers, oregano and coriander. Mexican and Southern style dishes regularly use chili powder to give the food an extra kick.

7. **Curry Powder** – Curry powder is a great spice to have on hand if you like spicy dishes

8. **Salt** – The most basic spice on this list, salt is a must have in most kitchens. There are several types of salt, including table salt and kosher salt, and even salt substitutes for those individuals who cannot for one reason or another consume traditional salt.

9. **Ground Cinnamon** – Cinnamon is a common ingredient in dessert dishes, such as cookies and cakes, and is even found in curries and various other recipes.

10. **Basil** – One of the least basic ingredients, basil is a flavorful and aromatic spice that can bring a one-of-a-kind taste to any dish. It can be used dried or fresh, and is even used as a garnish.

ΛΛΛΛΛΛΛΛΛΛΛΛΛΛΛΛΛΛΛΛΛΛΛΛΛΛΛΛΛΛΛΛΛΛΛΛΛΛΛΛΛΛΛΛΛΛΛΛΛΛΛ

# (2) Spice Shopping List

While the below list isn't the end all list of spices, it is a good list to start with. The following spices are commonly used in a wide array of spice blends and seasoning mixes. Feel free to add or eliminate any spices to the list.

- All spice
- Basil, dried
- Bay leaves
- Black pepper
- Brown sugar
- Cane sugar
- Cardamon
- Cayenne pepper
- Celery seeds
- Chili powder
- Cloves
- Cilantro
- Cinnamon
- Coriander
- Cumin
- Dill weed

- Garlic, fresh
- Garlic, powder
- Ginger, fresh
- Ginger, powder
- Lemon peels, dried
- Lemon pepper
- Lemon powder
- Nutmeg
- Onion powder
- Oregano
- Paprika
- Parsley
- Pepper flakes
- Rosemary, dried
- Sage, dried
- Thyme
- Turmeric
- White pepper
- White sugar

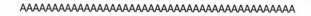

# (3) Storing Spices

Once you have your spice mixes and seasoning blend made, you will need to store them. As discussed in the beginning of the chapter, the spice mixes will need to be placed in an airtight container. These containers should be clearly labeled with the name of the mix or blend, as well as the date that you created the mix or blend. Once you have that taken care of, you will need to store the spice-filled jars in a cool dry location that is away from direct sunlight and direct heat. Not storing the spices properly will result in them spoiling faster and losing their flavor. Furthermore, you should routinely check the blends and seasoning to ensure they are still good to use. A good general rule of thumb is that you can keep homemade spices, mixes, blends and seasonings for 3 to 6 months. Smelling and tasting the spice mixture can typically give you a good idea of whether it is still useable. If the mix maintains its aroma and taste, it's probably still okay to use. If, however, the mix is dull with little to no aroma or taste, it's best to discard the mix and create a new batch.

AAAAAAAAAAAAAAAAAAAAAAAAAAAAAAAAAAAAAAAAAAAAAAAA

# Chapter X: The Different Types of Spices

AAAAAAAAAAAAAAAAAAAAAAAAAAAAAAAAAAAAAAAAAAAAAAAAAA

# (1) Common Spices

Spices in this category are regularly used by people all over the world and are generally a blend of various other individual spices. Because of this, these spice blends vary widely and typically contain spices from various parts of the world.

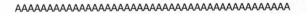

# (2) Culinary Spices and Herbs

Spices and herbs in this category are mainly used in the preparation of drinks and foods. Many times, culinary spices and herbs are subcategorized as botanical spices (see below).

AAAAAAAAAAAAAAAAAAAAAAAAAAAAAAAAAAAAAAAAAAAAAAAAAA

# (3) Botanical Spices

Botanical spices are made from plant based source, such as dried seeds/fruits, barks, roots, vegetables and fruits. They are commonly used for coloring, flavoring and natural food preservation. A few common spices in this category include:

- Dried seeds/fruits: nutmeg, mustard, black pepper and fennel
- Barks: Cassia (Chinese cinnamon) and cinnamon
- Roots: Ginger, galingale and turmeric
- Dried flowers: Cloves

# (4) Spices for Health

Throughout history, spices have played an important role in health. In fact, most spices hold some sort of medicinal use, and plants have act as medicine for even the earliest cultures. The most common spices used for their health benefits include:

Turmeric: This is one of the most well documented and studied spices, and it is well known for its medicinal properties. It is said to benefit a wide array of health problems and conditions including, arthritis, irritable bowel syndrome (IBS) and cystic fibrosis. Turmeric has also shown to prevent heart disease, restrict cancer growth, act as a cancer prevention and lower cholesterol levels. The curcumin naturally found in turmeric makes this spice a beneficial anti-viral and anti-inflammatory.

Cinnamon: Cinnamon isn't just a seasonal favorite flavor; it has shown to help treat a wide array of health conditions, such as regulate blood sugar, act as a cancer prevention, lower cholesterol, help treat yeast infections, promote brain health, relief pain symptoms associated with arthritis, act as an anti-clotting agent and fight E. Coli. Cinnamon is also a natural anti-bacterial and is high in nutrients.

Cayenne Pepper: Capsaicin, a component naturally found in cayenne pepper, is well known for its ability to alieve pain, reduce inflammation and act as an antioxidant. Capsaicin is such a respected pain reliever that it is often used as a main ingredient in over-the-counter pain medicine. Pain associated with psoriasis and arthritis typically benefits the most from cayenne pepper. Some studies have even suggested that cayenne pepper can also help reduce the risk of tumors.

Ginger: I am sure you have heard that sipping ginger ale can help relieve upset stomachs. So it's no surprise that ginger can help treat a wide array of digestive issues. In fact, pregnant women can safely take ginger to help alleviate morning sickness. Studies have also shown that ginger has anti-inflammatory properties.

AAAAAAAAAAAAAAAAAAAAAAAAAAAAAAAAAAAAAAAAAAAAAAA

# About the Author

Molly Mills always knew she wanted to feed people delicious food for a living. Being the oldest child with three younger brothers, Molly learned to prepare meals at an early age to help out her busy parents. She just seemed to know what spice went with which meat and how to make sauces that would dress up the blandest of pastas. Her creativity in the kitchen was a blessing to a family where money was tight and making new meals every day was a challenge.

Molly was also a gifted athlete as well as chef and secured a Lacrosse scholarship to Syracuse University. This was a blessing to her family as she was the first to go to college and at little cost to her parents. She took full advantage of her college education and earned a business degree. When she graduated, she joined her culinary skills and business acumen into a successful catering business. She wrote her first e-book after a customer asked if she could pay for several of her recipes. This sparked the entrepreneurial spirit in Mills and she thought if one person wanted them, then why not share the recipes with the world!

Molly lives near her family's home with her husband and three children and still cooks for her family every chance she gets. She plays Lacrosse with a local team made up of her old teammates from college and there are always some tasty nibbles on the ready after each game.

# Don't Miss Out!

Scan the QR-Code below and you can sign up to receive emails whenever Molly Mills publishes a new book. There's no charge and no obligation.

*Sign Me Up*

*https://molly.gr8.com*

CPSIA information can be obtained
at www.ICGtesting.com
Printed in the USA
LVHW090019090719
623524LV00001B/13/P